Original title:
Fibonacci Feelings

Copyright © 2024 Creative Arts Management OÜ
All rights reserved.

Author: Helena Marchant
ISBN HARDBACK: 978-9916-90-640-8
ISBN PAPERBACK: 978-9916-90-641-5

Serendipity in the Sequence

In the dance of fate we sway,
Moments collide, then drift away.
Serendipity's gentle hand,
Guides our steps through life's vast land.

Echoes whisper in the night,
Guiding us toward the light.
Paths entwined, yet free to roam,
In this chaos, we find home.

Petals of Progression

Softly blooming in the sun,
Each small step, a journey begun.
Petals fall, yet roots stay strong,
Nature's rhythm, a timeless song.

Seasons change and colors blend,
Through each twist, our souls ascend.
In the garden, hope remains,
Fertile ground where love sustains.

A Fibonacci Heartbeat

In sequences of life we find,
Patterns woven, beautifully entwined.
Each heartbeat, a number, a sign,
In the spiral, connection divine.

Nature's code in sacred form,
Guides us through every storm.
With each pulse, we grow and weave,
In this tapestry, we believe.

Hearts Unraveled in Order

Threads of love, so gently frayed,
In the fabric of life, we've played.
Hearts unraveled, yet aligned,
Beauty finds a way to bind.

In the chaos, find the peace,
In the unraveling, our release.
Through every twist, our story flows,
Connected still, love always grows.

Steps of Serene Growth

From seed to sprout, the journey starts,
With gentle rains, and warming hearts.
Each leaf unfurls, a tale to tell,
In quiet corners, where shadows dwell.

Through sunlit days and cooler nights,
The roots spread deep, embracing sights.
A dance of time, both calm and bold,
In nature's arms, our dreams unfold.

The Rhythm of Recurrence

In cycles spun, the seasons change,
Where frost and bloom both feel so strange.
A whisper soft in autumn's breath,
And echoes heard from life to death.

The moon will rise, the tides will flow,
Each dawn awakens, a chance to grow.
In twilight's hold, the stars reveal,
A timeless song, forever real.

Harmonies in Arithmetic

In numbers seen, a beauty lies,
With shapes that dance beneath the skies.
From angles sharp to circles round,
In every line, a truth is found.

The sum of parts, a greater whole,
In fractions small, we seek the role.
Patterns traced in nature's art,
Each equation sings, a vital part.

Love's Measured Journey

In quiet glances, hearts collide,
With every step, we're side by side.
Through winding roads, our stories blend,
In moments shared, our lives extend.

With every laugh and whispered sigh,
We chart a path beneath the sky.
In tender notes, each heartbeat plays,
A symphony through all our days.

The Heart's Spiral Path

In twilight's glow, we wander slow,
Through shadows deep, our secrets keep.
Each step we take, the echoes break,
A dance of souls, where time extols.

With each embrace, we find our place,
In swirling dreams, in silver beams.
The heart's soft call, unites us all,
On paths unknown, together grown.

Awe in Ascent

Above the clouds, where silence shrouds,
We climb the heights, towards wondrous sights.
The air is clear, the dawn draws near,
With every breath, we conquer death.

As mountains rise, we touch the skies,
A symphony, of hearts set free.
In vast expanse, we seek our chance,
To find the grace in nature's face.

The Spiral of Togetherness

In circles wide, we stand beside,
A tapestry, of you and me.
With threads so fine, our souls entwine,
In love's embrace, we find our place.

Through every turn, new lessons learn,
As seasons change, our hearts arrange.
In laughter shared, we find we're paired,
A spiral bright, our guiding light.

Arithmetic of Affection

In quiet sums, where love becomes,
A gentle touch, that means so much.
With every glance, we find our chance,
To solve the art, that ties the heart.

A simple score, of evermore,
Together strong, we both belong.
In numbers sweet, our lives complete,
The math of two, in love so true.

Ascending Affection

In the morning light, we rise anew,
Hearts entwined under skies so blue.
Each whispered word, a gentle spark,
Illuminating love's sweet arc.

Through valleys deep and mountains high,
Together we soar, just you and I.
With every step, our spirits blend,
A journey sweet that will not end.

Nature's Numerical Embrace

One leaf falls softly to the ground,
Two hearts race with a joyful sound.
Three stars twinkle in the night,
Four hopes soar, reaching for height.

Five flowers bloom in a vibrant dance,
Six wishes whispered in a glance.
Seven colors paint the dawn,
Eight threads of fate, in love, we're drawn.

Love in the Sequence

One glance, and the world stands still,
Two souls merge with a shared thrill.
Three dreams weave in a cosmic light,
Four seasons shaping our love right.

Five paths converge at destiny's gate,
Six heartbeats echo, it's never too late.
Seven promises softly spoken,
Eight lives intertwined, bonds unbroken.

Rhythms of Desire

In the quiet night, our hearts align,
With every breath, a sacred sign.
The pulse of longing beats so clear,
A melody only we can hear.

With every touch, the universe sways,
In waves of passion, our souls blaze.
Together we dance, in shadows and light,
Writing our story, pure and bright.

Patterns of Love

In colors bright, we weave our thread,
With whispered dreams, where hearts are led.
A tapestry of soft embrace,
In every stitch, we find our place.

Through seasons change, our laughter flows,
In gentle light, our garden grows.
With hands entwined, we share the song,
In every note, where we belong.

Echoes in the Spiral

A dance of light in shadows deep,
In whispered thoughts, our secrets keep.
The spiral spins, a tale so bright,
In every turn, we chase the light.

Through corridors of time and space,
Our spirits meet, a warm embrace.
In echoes soft, the past still sings,
Together we soar on crystal wings.

Counting the Waves of the Heart

Each wave that crashes, tells a tale,
In rhythm strong, we will not fail.
The sea of dreams spreads wide and far,
Guided by love, like a northern star.

With each new tide, our hopes arise,
Reflections dance in moonlit skies.
Counting the waves, our spirits rise,
In every splash, a sweet surprise.

Symmetry of Souls

In perfect balance, we align,
Two hearts as one, a sacred sign.
With mirrored thoughts, our dreams entwine,
In every glance, a glimpse divine.

Through thick and thin, together whole,
In harmony, we find our role.
The symmetry sings, a lovely tune,
In daylight bright or under the moon.

Tides of Affection

Waves crash softly on the shore,
Whispers of love forevermore.
Each tide carries a gentle sigh,
In the embrace where dreams lie.

The moon pulls hearts under its glow,
Like currents where warm feelings flow.
With every pulse, we drift and sway,
In this dance, we find our way.

The Arch of Connection

Beneath the arch, we meet and share,
A bond that blooms, tender and rare.
In laughter's echo, our spirits blend,
A bridge of trust that will not bend.

Hands intertwined, we walk as one,
Through shadows cast by the setting sun.
Every step a story, every glance,
In the arch of love, we take our chance.

Curved Reflections

In still waters, faces align,
Glances meet, two hearts entwine.
The curve of time shapes our trust,
In mirrored depths, it's love we must.

Ripples spread from every thought,
In reflections, lessons are taught.
Together, we dive into dreams,
In the curves, life's beauty gleams.

Blossoms in a Sequence

Petals unfold, a vibrant show,
In nature's dance, together we grow.
Each bloom a promise, bright and new,
In the garden of hearts, we nurture true.

The fragrance lingers, sweet and light,
In the daylight, we find our flight.
A sequence of moments, intertwined,
In every blossom, love we find.

The Language of Growth

In the garden, roots entwine,
Seeds are sown with careful hand.
Time whispers in soft design,
Nature speaks, we understand.

Leaves stretch up towards the sky,
Reaching out for light and grace.
Through the whispers, winds will sigh,
Growth takes time, but finds its place.

With each season comes a change,
Petals fall and new ones bloom.
Life's a dance, both sweet and strange,
Embracing all through joy and gloom.

Beneath the surface, strength is found,
Life's resilience knows no end.
In every loss, new dreams abound,
In every heart, a chance to mend.

Embracing Life's Patterns

Swirling leaves in autumn's dance,
Cycles fade and cycles flow.
In each moment, take a chance,
Let the patterns guide you slow.

Seasons shift with graceful ease,
Every heartbeat marks a thread.
Nature whispers through the trees,
Life's a tapestry we spread.

Find the rhythm, find your song,
In the chaos, seek the calm.
Though the road may seem so long,
Trust the process, hold the balm.

In every shadow, light will grow,
Embrace the cycles, find your way.
Life's sweet flow, a gentle flow,
In every night lies a new day.

A Weaving of Souls

Threads of fate and ties unseen,
In the loom, our lives combine.
Through the fabric, love is gleaned,
Woven close, our hearts align.

Stories told in silent eyes,
Every glance a gentle thread.
In shared laughter, joy will rise,
In sorrow, tender words are said.

Together in this vast expanse,
Each connection, precious, rare.
In the dance of life's sweet chance,
We find solace, we find care.

As we weave, our souls will blend,
Stronger with each moment shared.
In this tapestry, we mend,
In this love, we are snared.

Connections in Chaos

Amid the stormy nights, we find,
Woven threads that softly bind.
In whispers low, our souls unite,
Shining bright, a guiding light.

Through tangled paths, we weave our way,
In chaos found, we choose to stay.
Hands reaching out, in dark we trust,
In bonds of love, we rise from dust.

Among the noise, our hearts still beat,
Finding solace where shadows meet.
In every clash, a spark ignites,
Connections bloom, in moonlit sights.

Through shifting sands and restless seas,
We hold on tight to memories.
In every clash, we find our grace,
In chaos borne, our heart's embrace.

Heartbeats in a Spiral

Twisting gently, round we go,
In dances slow, our spirits flow.
With every turn, a breath we take,
In whispered dreams, our hearts awake.

Spiraling deeper, we find our way,
Through every night, into the day.
In circles drawn, our tales entwine,
A rhythm feels like yours and mine.

Each heartbeat echoes in the dark,
A soft melody, a gentle spark.
In shared warmth, we learn to trust,
In every sigh, a promise just.

As time unfolds, the love we share,
Draws us closer with tender care.
In spiral paths, together we grow,
A dance of hearts, a sacred flow.

The Art of Growing Together

In gardens lush, our roots run deep,
With care and time, we sow and reap.
Each tender shoot, a promise made,
In sunlight's kiss, our fears allayed.

Through seasons changing, hand in hand,
In storms we stand, together we'll stand.
Nurtured dreams in a shared embrace,
In every smile, our sacred space.

The art of growth, a dance of souls,
In unity, we become whole.
Like vines that climb, we touch the skies,
With every step, we rise and rise.

As blossoms bloom, we greet the dawn,
A tapestry where love has shone.
In every moment, forever tied,
The art of growing, side by side.

Numbers in the Breeze

In whispered sums, the secrets lie,
Counting stars that fill the sky.
Each number dances, light and free,
In hidden forms, a mystery.

From one to ten, the stories weave,
In every digit, dreams believe.
A gentle breeze carries the sound,
Of life's equations all around.

With every heartbeat, pulse a count,
In rhythms deep, our joys surmount.
In perfect harmony, we play,
Numbers guiding us every day.

In moonlit nights, they come alive,
In cosmic realms, we learn to thrive.
With hearts aligned, we feel the ease,
As we subtract our woes, like leaves.

Waves of Affection

Gentle whispers on the shore,
Carry love, forevermore.
Each tide brings a sweet embrace,
In the warmth of your grace.

Moments linger in the sand,
Hold my heart with tender hand.
Ripples spark with every glance,
In this timeless, loving dance.

When the storm begins to rise,
Through the chaos, see the skies.
Your voice calms the raging sea,
Waves of love, eternally.

In the moonlight's silver glow,
Feel the currents softly flow.
As the ocean meets the night,
Our hearts blend in pure delight.

Cycles of Yearning

Spring awakens hopes anew,
Fresh blossoms, vibrant hue.
Underneath the warming sun,
Yearning hearts beat as one.

Summer's heat ignites the fire,
Passions bloom and dreams aspire.
Every glance a spark of fate,
Lost in time, we await.

Autumn leaves begin to fall,
Whispers echo through it all.
Moments fade like fading light,
Yet, the yearning feels so right.

Winter's chill may seal the day,
Yet inside, the heart's ballet.
Cycles turn, but love will stay,
Yearning grows in a soft way.

The Growth of an Emotion

A seed planted deep within,
Nurtured soft, where dreams begin.
Roots entwine, they hold so tight,
In the dark, seeking the light.

Leaves unfurl, they greet the sun,
Every moment feels like fun.
In this garden, hearts will grow,
Love in colors, bright and slow.

Weathered storms, they come and go,
Yet the bond continues to flow.
With each tear, a blossom blooms,
From shadows, life forever looms.

Time will gift a fragrant air,
Emotions flourish everywhere.
Together we'll face every season,
In love's garden, we've found reason.

Dimensions of Desire

In the silence, whispers play,
Around the thoughts, words will sway.
Desire sparks like constellations,
Filling voids, igniting sensations.

Entwined minds in sweet delight,
Every glance a spark of light.
Through the layers, depth we find,
Love expands, two hearts aligned.

In the shadows, passions bloom,
Filling spaces, breaking gloom.
Dimensions dance, a playful tease,
In the warmth, we find our ease.

Time is but a fleeting phase,
With each breath, the heart's ablaze.
In this world where dreams converge,
Desire flows, and souls emerge.

Growth Through Patterns

Seeds in the ground, they take their time,
Roots intertwine, a dance so prime.
Weather and sun, they play their part,
In silent grace, they nurture the heart.

Branches extend, reaching the sky,
Windsong whispers, as they sigh.
Patience teaches, day by day,
In every rhythm, they find their way.

The Radiance of Relationships

In laughter shared, a bond is formed,
In silent moments, love is warmed.
Through trials faced and joy embraced,
Together we shine, every path traced.

Hands that hold with gentle might,
Hearts that beat, a shared delight.
In every glance, a story told,
A tapestry woven, rich and bold.

Emotions in a Curve

Waves of joy crash on the shore,
While shadows weave, a tale of lore.
Peaks of laughter, valleys of tears,
In every bend, the heart steers clear.

Colors swirl in a tempest dance,
Whispers echo, a fleeting chance.
Emotions rise and fall like tide,
In this curve, our truths abide.

Patterns of the Heart

In every beat, a rhythm flows,
Mapping paths where love bestows.
Lines drawn softly, in trust we meet,
In patterns formed, our hearts entreat.

Moments linger, like a sigh,
In shadows cast, we learn to fly.
Colors blend in soft embrace,
In every heart, a sacred space.

Patterns in the Wilderness

In the forest where shadows play,
Leaves whisper secrets of the day.
Twisted branches form a frame,
Nature holds its wild acclaim.

Footprints echo on the ground,
Silent stories all around.
Colors weave in a gentle dance,
Life unfolds with every chance.

Ripples run through open streams,
Reflecting sunlight in bright gleams.
Winds carry tales of distant lands,
In the wild, a freedom stands.

The Art of Growing Affection

In the garden where soft hearts bloom,
Love takes root amidst the gloom.
Each tender leaf whispers trust,
Nurtured by hope, and love is a must.

Petals open with a fragrant sigh,
Underneath the vast, blue sky.
Together we weather every storm,
In the warmth, our spirits form.

Hands entwined like ivy's embrace,
Growing closer in every space.
Time tends to our sacred ground,
In this love, we are truly found.

Spirals of Emotion

In the depths where feelings swirl,
Hearts spin in a tender whirl.
Joy and sorrow intertwine,
Life's essence in every line.

Laughter dances like pure light,
While shadows linger through the night.
Caught in a loop, we rise and fall,
Emotion's spiral, we embrace all.

Each moment a thread we weave,
In love's tapestry, we believe.
Endless cycles shaping our fate,
Spirals of emotion, never too late.

The Golden Ratio Heart

In the heart where beauty lies,
Symmetry beneath the skies.
Curves that flow like gentle streams,
Crafting life from vibrant dreams.

With every beat, a rhythm flows,
Nature's pattern, endless prose.
A cadence found in every part,
Essence balanced, a work of art.

Love aligns with perfect grace,
In this harmonious embrace.
Life's design, a sacred chart,
Guided by the golden heart.

Dances of Delight

In the fields where shadows play,
Joyful hearts find their way.
Laughter twirls in the sun's embrace,
Every step a light-filled race.

Colors blend in a waltz of hues,
Under skies where freedom brews.
Dancing feet on the soft, warm ground,
In every rhythm, love is found.

Moments spin like leaves in flight,
Chasing dreams through day and night.
The air is sweet with fragrant cheer,
In this dance, all sorrow's clear.

Together we feel the music's spark,
In the glow of the day turning dark.
As stars emerge in the evening sky,
Our hearts join in, forever to fly.

The Maze of Emotion

Winding paths of joy and pain,
Each corner hides a flowing vein.
Moments linger, shadows creep,
In the maze, we sometimes weep.

Hope is bright like the morning sun,
But doubts can cloud what's just begun.
Finding peace in a tangled thread,
Mapping dreams where fears once tread.

Joyful laughter, a sudden flare,
Turns to silence, a broken prayer.
Twisting turns that lead us astray,
Yet, we search for the light of day.

In the heart, a compass beats,
Guiding us through life's complex streets.
Through every twist, love's beacon shines,
In this maze, our fate aligns.

Letters in a Spiral

Ink flows like a gentle stream,
Words curl softly, weave a dream.
Letters dance on paper's face,
In swirling scripts, we find our place.

Messages wrapped in tender folds,
Secrets shared, courage unfolds.
Whispers linger, soft as night,
In every curve, a spark of light.

Time encapsulated in each line,
Moments captured, yours and mine.
Through spirals of feeling, truth is drawn,
In quiet corners, night meets dawn.

Each letter holds a piece of soul,
Binding hearts as they make us whole.
In this spiral, we twist and turn,
For every page, a flame to burn.

Harmonic Bloom

Petals open, colors bright,
In the garden, pure delight.
Chorus sings of spring's sweet song,
Where our hearts will always belong.

Nature's brush paints every hue,
Underneath the vast, blue view.
Harmony flows in each soft breeze,
Inhale deeply, we find our ease.

Buzzing bees and birds that glide,
In this beauty, we confide.
Every bloom a tale to tell,
In its fragrance, we dwell.

Time unfolds with every day,
In this moment, come what may.
In harmonic waves, we shall trust,
Blooming together, love is a must.

The Beauty of Balance

In nature's rhythm we find our peace,
A delicate dance of give and cease.
Light and shadow entwine so tight,
Creating harmony, day and night.

A scale that tips with gentle grace,
Each element finds its rightful place.
With every breath, we strive to blend,
The beauty of balance, our true friend.

In storms we learn to stand our ground,
As tides of fortune come around.
Through highs and lows, we learn to sway,
Embracing balance each new day.

Let nature teach us to align,
In every heartbeat, you'll find the sign.
A perfect poise, a graceful art,
The beauty of balance in every heart.

Embracing Curves

In every curve, a story flows,
Shapes of beauty, soft and slow.
Winding paths that gently tease,
Embracing curves, we find our ease.

Like rivers bending through the land,
Sculpting dreams with nature's hand.
In every twist, there's magic spun,
A journey's trace, the race begun.

Each gentle arc a call to roam,
A silhouette that feels like home.
In lush embrace, we come alive,
Celebrating curves, we thrive and strive.

The art of life in every bend,
In curves we trust, we start to mend.
With open hearts, we learn to flow,
In every curve, our spirits grow.

Layers of Connection

Beneath the surface, stories hide,
Layers of connection, side by side.
In shadows deep, we find the light,
Unraveling ties both day and night.

Through whispers soft and laughter loud,
We build our bridges, steady and proud.
Each moment shared, a thread we weave,
In vibrant patterns, we believe.

The dance of hearts in close embrace,
Binds us together in this space.
In layers rich, we find our voice,
In every bond, we make a choice.

So tenderly we touch and feel,
In every layer, love is real.
Together in this endless quest,
Layers of connection, we are blessed.

The Dance of Numbers

One leads the way, a solitary path,
Two brings the joy, a shared laugh.
Three spins a tale of harmony,
Four creates a stable symphony.

In every digit, a rhythm sweet,
Patterns emerge, a flowing beat.
Five raises hands, inviting in,
Six brings the charm, where dreams begin.

Counting stars in the velvet night,
Each number dances in pure delight.
Seven weaves magic, eight takes flight,
The beauty of digits, shining bright.

With every sum, we find our place,
In the dance of numbers, a warm embrace.
Together we create, forever inspire,
The dance of numbers, a burning fire.

Sentiments in the Fibonacci Garden

In the garden where numbers grow,
Petals open, secrets flow.
Spirals twist in nature's art,
Each bloom a whisper of the heart.

Golden ratio, a song unfolds,
With every curve, a tale is told.
Colors dance in sunlight's grace,
Life reflects in each soft face.

Time unwinds in gentle folds,
Moments captured, memories hold.
Nature sings in harmony,
In Fibonacci's symphony.

Feelings blend in vibrant hues,
From every stem, a love renews.
In this garden, we shall find,
The union of heart and mind.

Synchronized Rhythms

Hearts in sync, a muted drum,
Footsteps blend, a soft hum.
Twilight's glow dances near,
A silent bond, pure and clear.

Waves of sound, they ebb and flow,
Like whispers in the wind that blow.
Each heartbeat matches time's embrace,
Together forging our own space.

Music weaves through every sigh,
Underneath the vast, endless sky.
Hands entwined, we gently sway,
In the rhythm of this day.

Through the night, our laughter's tune,
Guided softly by the moon.
Close your eyes, feel the beat,
In love's dance, we're complete.

The Spiral Staircase of Love

Each step we take winds higher still,
Curving softly, hearts to fill.
With every turn, a promise shared,
In the spiral, we've dared.

Hand in hand, we rise and fall,
Whispers echo, love's sweet call.
Moments linger, shadows play,
In this staircase, we shall stay.

Reaching heights no fear can find,
In each step, our souls aligned.
Through the winding, we embrace,
Finding joy in every space.

At the top, a view so grand,
Together still, we make our stand.
In the spiral, love's design,
Endless journey, yours and mine.

Transforming Numbers into Feelings

Count the stars, wish on each light,
Transforming numbers into flight.
Every digit, a tale to weave,
Emotions live in what we believe.

One to three, hearts entwined,
Two to five, love defined.
Six blooms bright, the season's change,
In each count, we rearrange.

The sums of laughter, tears we share,
In every fraction, we find care.
Equations solve in evening's glow,
In numbers, our feelings grow.

Let's add the moments, subtract our fears,
In this math, we'll find our years.
With every total, dreams will rise,
Transforming numbers into skies.

Petals Unfolding

In the morning light, petals bloom,
Soft whispers of nature, dispelling gloom.
Colors awaken, brightening the day,
Fragile beauty dances, in gentle sway.

With each drop of dew, dreams come alive,
Fragrant secrets in the air, they thrive.
Nature's canvas painted in vibrant hues,
Every unfolding moment, a world to choose.

Beneath the sun's gaze, life's stories unfold,
With every breath taken, new tales are told.
In gardens of presence, the heart finds its way,
Embracing the now, come what may.

As twilight descends, colors start to fade,
Yet in every shadow, hope is laid.
Petals, like memories, drift on the breeze,
A reminder of love that puts the heart at ease.

Love's Recursive Journey

We start with a glance, a spark in the air,
Entwined in a dance, a moment to share.
With whispers of laughter, our hearts intertwine,
An endless adventure, a path so divine.

Through valleys of doubt, we wander and roam,
Each step brings us closer, we're never alone.
In echoes of trust, our shadows align,
The rhythm of love plays, a tune so fine.

Seasons may change, but our love remains true,
In each twist of fate, I'm drawn back to you.
Through trials and triumphs, together we stand,
In the tapestry of time, we weave hand in hand.

With every embrace, we journey anew,
In the circle of love, it's just me and you.
A recursive embrace, ever deepening grace,
In the heart's sacred space, our souls find their place.

Golden Threads of Emotion

Woven through time, golden threads of grace,
In the fabric of life, each moment we trace.
With the warmth of a smile, soft and sincere,
In the tapestry of feeling, love draws us near.

Each thread tells a story, both joy and despair,
In the colors of longing, we find treasures rare.
Frayed edges of sorrow, mended with care,
Through the loom of our hearts, we stitch our share.

As sunlight dances on delicate seams,
Our dreams intertwine, weaving vibrant themes.
With every heartbeat, we honor the flow,
In the quilt of existence, our spirits will grow.

In the embrace of time, a rich blend unfolds,
With every woven moment, the heart softly molds.
Golden threads of emotion, forever they bind,
A legacy of love, in the fabric we find.

Patterns Woven in Time

In the whispers of ages, patterns arise,
Guiding our footsteps beneath endless skies.
Threads of our stories, intricately sewn,
Moments we cherish, memories grown.

Through seasons that change, we dance on their flow,
Each heartbeat a marker, a tale we both know.
In labyrinths woven with shadows and light,
Our journey unfolds, ever bold in its flight.

With each twist and turn, new visions appear,
In the mosaic of life, we embrace what is dear.
From laughter to tears, in rhythms we bind,
In the patterns of time, our hearts intertwine.

As we sketch our future, with colors so bright,
Creating a canvas, reflecting our light.
Together, we craft what each moment can be,
In the patterns of time, forever we're free.

Rhymes of the Right Angles

In corners where shadows softly play,
Angles meet in a dance, night and day.
Symmetry whispers, a geometric song,
Lines intersect, where we all belong.

Each vertex holds secrets of silent grace,
Squares and triangles find their place.
Through math we speak, a language so clear,
In right angles we cherish, we hold dear.

With rulers and compasses, we draw our fate,
Blueprints of destinies patiently wait.
In harmony, shapes collide and combine,
Layouts of life on the endless design.

So let us embrace each angle and line,
In the geometry of hearts, we'll forever shine.

Loops of Longing

In circles we wander, hearts intertwined,
Spirals of yearning, souls unconfined.
The echo of laughter, a sweet serenade,
In the loops of our dreams, love is displayed.

Time dances round us, a playful embrace,
In infinite loops, we find our place.
With every heartbeat, we spiral anew,
Longing entwined in the moments we view.

So let us keep turning, through shadow and gleam,
In the circles of life, we follow our dream.
Paths overlap, in a whimsical chase,
Forever entwined in longing's warm grace.

Through loops of existence, together we fly,
With love as our compass, we never say goodbye.

A Spiral of Dreams

In the depths of the night, dreams gently weave,
A spiral of visions, we dare to believe.
With each turn we take, hearts start to glow,
In the dance of the soul, we ebb and flow.

Stars twinkle above, guiding our way,
Through the spiral of time, night turns to day.
Whispers of hope in the soft morning light,
Together we journey, our futures ignite.

Each dream a petal, unfolding with grace,
In the garden of wishes, we each find our space.
Layers of longing, like rings on a tree,
In the spiral of dreams, we find you and me.

So let us keep dreaming, through thick and through thin,
In the spiral of life, let our adventure begin.

Nature's Love Map

Beneath the vast sky and the whispering trees,
Nature unveils her delicate keys.
With rivers as paths and mountains as guides,
In nature's love map, true beauty abides.

The breeze carries tales of love in the air,
Every flower and leaf knows how much we care.
With each rustling branch, each chirping song,
In the quiet of nature, we truly belong.

Sunset paints colors that warm the heart,
In nature's embrace, we never part.
With stars that illuminate the darkest night,
We follow the map, it leads us to light.

So wander with me through this wild expanse,
In nature's love map, let's take a chance.
With every footprint, and every shared glance,
We'll chart our own course, in this joyful dance.

Conch Shells and Heartbeats

Whispers of the ocean call,
Within the shell, I hear it all.
Each heartbeat echoes, strong and clear,
The rhythm of life drawing near.

Tides rise and fall, the dance of fate,
In every pulse, I contemplate.
Conch shells hold secrets of the sea,
In their embrace, I find my peace.

Sand beneath my wandering feet,
Nature's song, so pure and sweet.
The conch, my guide to tranquil shores,
Where heartbeats blend with ocean roars.

In silence, listen, truth unfolds,
Through whispered hearts and stories told.
A journey where the soul can dwell,
In the rhythm of conchs and heartbeats swell.

The Universe in Each Beat

Every heartbeat speaks of light,
A universe in endless night.
Stars align within my chest,
In the calm, I find my rest.

Galaxies spiral in my dreams,
Each pulse ignites the cosmic beams.
A symphony of distant skies,
In every beat, the cosmos lies.

Time transcends with every sound,
Within my heart, the space is found.
A gentle thrum, a stardust song,
In this rhythm, I belong.

Eternal wonders in the heart,
The universe a work of art.
As I breathe and feel each spark,
In every beat, I touch the dark.

Spiraled Sentiments

Feelings twist like autumn leaves,
In every swirl, my heart believes.
Spirals of joy and pain entwined,
Emotions dance within my mind.

In shadows cast and sunlight glows,
The depth of love and sorrow grows.
Each twist reveals a hidden truth,
The innocence of cherished youth.

As spirals spiral, I learn to see,
The beauty in the fragility.
Each sentiment a tale to tell,
In the maze where feelings dwell.

With every turn that life presents,
I navigate these spiraled scents.
In every heartbeat, I reside,
With spiraled love as my guide.

Echoing Stardust

In the silence, stardust hums,
A melody of where it comes.
Through galaxies in twilight's glow,
The echoes of the night we know.

Softly drifting through the sky,
Wishes soar and dreams don't die.
In every sparkle, stories lay,
Echoing softly night and day.

Time will meld with cosmic grace,
Each heartbeat finds its rightful place.
In the vastness, souls unite,
Echoing stardust, pure delight.

Listen closely, hear the call,
In stardust echoes, we are all.
Connected by the warmth of light,
In every heartbeat, pure insight.

The Heart's Algorithm

In rhythms soft, our pulses blend,
A dance of fate, where love extends.
With whispered vows, we find the key,
Unlocking dreams, just you and me.

Through circuits drawn by stars above,
We calculate the math of love.
Each moment shared, a data trail,
In sync, our hearts shall never fail.

With every beat, the code refines,
Patterns emerge, a path defines.
In algorithms made for two,
Our heartbeats sync, forever true.

Together in this dance we choose,
In numbers vast, we cannot lose.
A symphony of what we are,
Your heart, my hands, our guiding star.

Harmonics of the Heart

In echoes soft, our hearts do play,
A melody that lights the way.
Each note a promise, warm and bright,
In harmony, we find our light.

With every chord, our spirits soar,
A song of love, forevermore.
Resonating in tender grace,
In unison, we find our place.

The rhythm flows, a sweet refrain,
In laughter shared, in joy, in pain.
Together, we compose our tune,
Beneath the watchful, silver moon.

Through whispered words, our symphony,
Unfurls like petals from a tree.
In harmonic truth, we reside,
Two hearts entwined, the perfect guide.

Geometry of Longing

In angles sharp, the shadows play,
The lines of love, they bend and sway.
With every glance, the shapes align,
In silent spaces, hearts combine.

The circle formed by whispered dreams,
In geometric arcs, love streams.
Each vertex holds a memory,
In every curve, our destiny.

With lengths that stretch across the night,
In measured beats, we find the light.
As polygons of soul embrace,
In this design, we find our place.

Bound by the angles we create,
In syntax pure, we navigate.
In this geometry, we trust,
Our hearts entwined, a bond robust.

A Sequence of Trust

In patterns formed, our hearts align,
A sequence built on yours and mine.
Each step we take, a promise made,
In bonds of trust, our fears allayed.

From silence shared, the roots will grow,
In tender gestures, love will show.
With every glance, our truth unfolds,
A story written, brave and bold.

As time progresses, faith will bloom,
In shadows cast, dispelling gloom.
The sequence flows, a gentle stream,
In trust, we find our deepest dream.

Together through the trials we face,
In unity, we find our grace.
A tapestry of heart and soul,
In this sequence, we are whole.

Golden Ratio of Longing

In shadows cast by evening glow,
Desires pulse like rivers flow.
A measure found in hearts' deep yearn,
As time reveals, we twist and turn.

The space between, a sacred thread,
In every glance, words left unsaid.
We share a dance, a silent song,
In perfect balance, where we belong.

Whispers of Growing Waves

The ocean calls with softest sighs,
A rhythm found where silence lies.
Together we embrace the tide,
As mysteries of depth abide.

In every swell, our spirits rise,
With dreams reborn beneath the skies.
The whispers echo through the air,
In this vast sea, we lay our care.

The Spiral Dance of Affection

With every turn, we find our fate,
In spirals drawn that captivate.
Entwined in grace, we sway and glide,
In harmony where hearts confide.

A gentle push, the ebb and flow,
In tender touch, our love will grow.
Each step we take, a promise shared,
In this sweet waltz, we're always paired.

Infinity in a Single Breath

In moments fleeting, time stands still,
A breath unfolds with quiet thrill.
Within this pause, eternity,
We taste the vastness, you and me.

The universe in our embrace,
A fleeting glance, a sacred space.
With every heartbeat, love's refrain,
We find forever in the pain.

Spirals of Emotion

In the depths of silence, feelings rise,
Whispers echo softly, beneath blue skies.
Twists and turns, the heart's own path,
Carving ways through joy and wrath.

Colors swirl in endless dance,
Every heartbeat a fleeting chance.
Ribbons of sorrow, waves of glee,
Entwined together, endlessly free.

Moments pulse, a vibrant glow,
An inner rhythm, steady flow.
Cascades of laughter, tears that gleam,
Life's tableau, a waking dream.

Through spirals we weave our tale,
In the tapestry of love, we sail.
With every spin, we learn, we grow,
Embracing the chaos, letting it flow.

The Sequence of Heartbeats

In the stillness, a rhythm begins,
Softly echoing, where life spins.
A steady thump, a dance of flesh,
Each pulse a promise, anew enmesh.

Seconds tick in syncopated rhyme,
In every heartbeat, a touch of time.
A melody formed beneath our skin,
Whispered secrets waiting to begin.

With fervent longing, the tempo sways,
In love's embrace, the heart obeys.
Beats entwined, a sacred vow,
Together we thrive, here and now.

The sequence flows, a song divine,
Chronicles of old, a moment's design.
In this cadence, we find our place,
In the heartbeat's depths, we trace our grace.

Patterns of the Soul

Underneath the surface, shadows play,
Patterns emerge in a subtle array.
Each thought a thread, a delicate weave,
In the fabric of being, we believe.

Geometric wonders, spirals that twist,
In every creation, moments persist.
The soul's own canvas, painted bright,
Reflecting the depths of day and night.

Guided by dreams, we form our way,
A symphony sung, a bright ballet.
Through the maze of our fears and desires,
We find the patterns, ignite our fires.

In every heartbeat, in every sigh,
The shapes of existence brush the sky.
With love as our compass, we'll find our goal,
Navigating through the patterns of the soul.

Nature's Numbered Embrace

Beneath the stars, where shadows play,
Nature whispers in her own way.
Counting the leaves on a quiet tree,
The rhythm of life in harmony.

Seasons shift, a timeless dance,
Numbers guide fate's gentle chance.
Each petal's fall, each bird's flight,
Nature's embrace, both tender and bright.

From mountains tall to rivers wide,
Every curve reflects a hidden guide.
Counting the waves that kiss the shore,
Life's fleeting moments, always want more.

So let us wander, hand in hand,
Through nature's beauty, beneath her stand.
In her numbered embrace, we'll find our place,
In the vastness of love, a warm embrace.

Infinite Whispers

In silent night, the stars will gleam,
Soft secrets dance, like a dream.
Echoes of time, they gently flow,
Infinite whispers, in moonlit glow.

Breezes carry tales unknown,
Across the sky, where wishes are sown.
Hearts converge, their hopes entwine,
A symphony sweet, so divine.

Fragments of time, they intertwine,
Memories linger, like aged wine.
In every breath, a story lives,
Infinite whispers, the night forgives.

Within the shadows, truths abide,
In quiet corners, love won't hide.
A bond unbroken, though worlds apart,
Infinite whispers, a timeless art.

The Petals of Time

In gardens lush, the petals fall,
Each one a moment, a soft call.
Time unfurls in colors bright,
A journey woven, day to night.

Fleeting hours, like blossoms bloom,
Fading softly, as shadows loom.
Carry the essence, let it shine,
In the dance of life, the petals align.

Seasons change, but love stays true,
Through storms and sunshine, it renews.
Embrace each day, let worries cease,
In the petals of time, find your peace.

So gather round, and share a smile,
In the garden's heart, stay awhile.
Each petal whispers a sacred rhyme,
In the beauty of life, the petals of time.

Unraveling the Spiral

In a world where shadows twine,
Unraveling the spiral, we start to shine.
With every twist, a truth to find,
In the dance of fate, our hearts aligned.

Journey unfolds, through light and dark,
A path of echoes, a sacred arc.
Every turn reveals a face,
In the spiral's grasp, we seek our place.

Trust the rhythm, let go of fear,
In the spiral's hug, the path is clear.
Unlock the heart, embrace the climb,
In unraveling tales, we beat in time.

Together we soar, on wings of gold,
In the stories untold, our dreams unfold.
Embrace the spiral, let your soul dive,
In the dance of life, we truly thrive.

When Hearts Align

In quiet moments, our souls confess,
When hearts align, we feel the blessed.
A spark ignites, a gentle glow,
Together we wander, where love can grow.

Through whispered dreams, we intertwine,
In every glance, our souls combine.
Time stands still, as stars align,
In this sacred space, your heart is mine.

Bound by hope and tender grace,
Life's journey shared, in this embrace.
Hand in hand, through thick and thin,
When hearts align, the light begins.

So trust the path, and take the chance,
In the dance of love, we find our stance.
A timeless bond, forever signed,
In the rhythm of life, when hearts align.

Love's Recurring Dream

In twilight's embrace, hearts entwine,
Whispers of secrets, a sacred sign.
Under the stars, we dance and sway,
Love's sweet echo, never fades away.

With every heartbeat, a tender spark,
Illuminating the journey, lighting the dark.
Promises whispered on soft summer nights,
In love's recurring dream, we take flight.

Through seasons we wander, hand in hand,
Each moment together, a beautiful strand.
Drawing us closer, our spirits unite,
Forever blooming in love's pure light.

As dawn gently breaks, we awake anew,
In the warmth of your gaze, the world feels true.
In love's recurring dream, we find our way,
Together, forever, come what may.

Echoes of a Spiral Journey

In the corridors of time, we roam free,
Chasing echoes of what's meant to be.
Spirals of laughter, moments we share,
A journey unfolding, beyond compare.

Each step we take, a story revealed,
Winding through memories, hearts unconcealed.
With every turn, our path intertwines,
In echoes of love, our destiny shines.

Through valleys of doubt, we forge ahead,
Carving our dreams, on hope we are fed.
With courage and grace, we rise and we learn,
In echoes of a spiral, we yearn and return.

Together we dance, in rhythm and rhyme,
Lost in the beauty of space and time.
With every heartbeat, our spirits align,
In echoes of a journey, so divine.

Symphony of Sequence

In the quiet of night, a melody plays,
Each note a heartbeat, in intricate sways.
Harmonies blossom, in structured embrace,
A symphony rising, a dance through space.

With rhythm and pulse, we sway in the light,
Entwined like shadows, a beautiful sight.
In sequences woven, our stories unfold,
A tapestry rich, with dreams to behold.

With every crescendo, we soar and we dive,
Alive in this moment, we truly thrive.
From silence to sonnet, our souls intertwine,
In the symphony of sequence, love is divine.

As day breaks anew, the echoes remain,
In the symphony played, we've cherished the gain.
A cycle of love, forever to keep,
In rhythm of hearts, our promise runs deep.

Choreography of Numbers

In a universe vast, where patterns collide,
Numbers like stars, in the cosmos they guide.
Each figure a story, a truth to convey,
In choreography written, in life's grand ballet.

With every equation, there's beauty described,
In angles and curves, a dance that's prescribed.
We twirl through the figures, each line a decree,
In the choreography of what's meant to be.

From zero to one, the journey begins,
In the realm of existence, where silence thins.
Through fractions and sums, we find our way clear,
In the numbers' embrace, we shed all our fear.

As the clock gently ticks, the dance flows with grace,
In a world full of numbers, we find our true place.
The choreography written in whispers of time,
In the rhythm of life, we soar and we climb.

Nature's Loving Mathematics

In whispers of trees, the secrets reveal,
Patterns of life, so gentle and real.
The rhythm of rivers, the pulse of the ground,
Nature's sweet numbers, in silence abound.

Fibonacci's spiral in petals we see,
A dance of equations in every green lea.
From mountains to valleys, the balance is shown,
In nature's embrace, our hearts find a home.

Aromas of Ascent

A waft of the jasmine, the peak of the hill,
Perfumed with the promise, the heart learns to thrill.
With every ascent, a new scent we find,
The essence of earth, in our souls intertwined.

Citrus and cedar, the air thick with grace,
Notes of our journeys, each step we embrace.
As we climb higher, the world falls away,
In the aroma of sky, our spirits will sway.

The Geometry of Love

In angles and shapes, our passions align,
A circle of trust, forever entwined.
Triangles of laughter, with sides that are true,
In the canvas of hearts, love sketches anew.

Ellipses of longing, we orbit so near,
Each point a reminder of why we are here.
With curves that enchant, our lives intertwined,
In the geometry of love, pure bliss we find.

Unraveling Time's Tenderness

In seconds that flutter like leaves on the breeze,
We capture the moments, our hearts find their ease.
With each tick of the clock, we learn to embrace,
The tenderness woven in time's softest lace.

Memories linger like echoes of song,
A dance through the ages where we all belong.
As the past intertwines with what's yet to be,
In unraveling time, we find our decree.

Echoes of Growing Moments

In a garden where shadows play,
Children laugh as their dreams sway,
Petals fall like whispered hopes,
As the sun dips, and daylight gropes.

Time writes stories in the air,
Moments cherished, seeds laid bare,
Each echo, a tender list,
A breath of past, never missed.

As seasons change and shadows fade,
Memories linger, softly laid,
In the heart, where stillness grows,
The life within forever glows.

Here we stand, both firm and free,
In the echoes, we find the key,
To treasures buried in the soul,
Guiding us to feel more whole.

A Math of Melancholy

Count the days in silent rows,
Each tick a seed the silence sows,
Numbers dance, a mournful song,
In the shadows, where hearts belong.

Subtraction leads to empty spaces,
Calculating what time erases,
Echoes linger of laughter lost,
In the quiet, we bear the cost.

Algebra of joy and pain,
X marks the spot where dreams remain,
In every problem, a tale unfolds,
A journey mapped in shades of gold.

Yet through the ache, we find our way,
In darker nights, a light will play,
Melancholy, a bittersweet friend,
In the math of life, we learn to mend.

Waves of Connection

Across the sea where whispers fly,
Hearts collide like waves nearby,
Each swell a bridge, a fleeting touch,
In the silence, we feel so much.

Rippling echoes of laughter shared,
In the tide of memories, we've dared,
Beneath the surface, currents flow,
Binding souls, more than we know.

As the moon pulls at the tide,
We dance through life, side by side,
Each wave a moment, sweet and true,
In the ocean, I find you.

Together, we rise, together we fall,
In waves of connection, we hear the call,
Embracing the flow, forever we blend,
In the rhythm of time, love knows no end.

The Curves of Yearning

In the embrace of twilight's glow,
Curves of longing begin to flow,
Whispers carried on a gentle breeze,
In the shadows, hearts find ease.

The arc of dreams, soft and wide,
Yearning souls, none can hide,
In the silence of an open sky,
We touch the stars, we learn to fly.

With every curve, a story spins,
In the depths where hope begins,
Tracing lines of what could be,
In each heartbeat, you're with me.

Love's gentle swirl, a sacred dance,
In the curves, we take our chance,
To intertwine, to weave, to yearn,
In every moment, together we learn.

Spiraling Echoes of Joy

In the dance of laughter's light,
Whispers twirl in pure delight,
Colors blend, horizons fade,
Echoes sing, the joy displayed.

Floating on the softest breeze,
Chasing dreams through swaying trees,
Hearts entwined in radiant glow,
Spiraling high where spirits flow.

Moments caught in gentle hands,
Build a world of sacred strands,
In each note, a vibrant sound,
In each heart, love's warmth is found.

Let the music lift us high,
Together, we will touch the sky,
Riding waves of blissful cheer,
Spiraling echoes, ever near.

The Spiral Staircase of Emotion

Every step leads hearts to climb,
Circles turn, transcending time,
Feelings rise and fall like tides,
In the spiral, truth abides.

Upward through the shadows cast,
Whispers of the loves we've passed,
Every twist, a lesson learned,
In the depths, our spirits yearned.

With each landing, fresh new views,
Bridges built, paths we can choose,
Winding tightly, hand in hand,
On this staircase, we will stand.

Embrace the curves, embrace the turns,
For every soul within us burns,
In this journey, we're not alone,
The spiral staircase leads us home.

Cycles of a Kindred Spirit

In the cycles, hearts align,
Rhythms beat, a dance divine,
Side by side, we roam the night,
Kindred souls in shared sunlight.

Seasons change, the world spins round,
In each pulse, our love is found,
Through the storms, we find our light,
Cycles weave our shared delight.

As the moon pulls at the sea,
So your spirit calls to me,
In the ebb and flow, we trust,
Cycles binding, love is a must.

Together, through the dark we stride,
In each heartbeat, friends abide,
Cycles of a kindred flame,
In this bond, we find our name.

Ascending Heartstrings

Gently plucked, our heartstrings twine,
Melodies they weave, divine,
Elevating dreams to soar,
In each note, we seek for more.

Through the echoes of the past,
Whispers linger, shadows cast,
Rising high on wings of song,
In this harmony, we belong.

As we climb the skyward path,
Finding joy despite the wrath,
Every chord a story told,
Ascending heartstrings, pure as gold.

Together, we embrace the climb,
Painting love in every rhyme,
In our music, hope ignites,
Ascending higher, pure delights.

Milton Keynes UK
Ingram Content Group UK Ltd.
UKHW020043271124
451585UK00012B/1031